Primary Sources of the Civil Rights Movement

John Lewis and Desegregation

Gerry Boehme

Cavendish Square

New York

Published in 2017 by Cavendish Square Publishing, LLC
243 5th Avenue, Suite 136, New York, NY 10016

CPSIA Compliance Information: Batch #CS16CSQ

All websites were available and accurate when this book was sent to press.

Library of Congress Cataloging-in-Publication Data

Names: Boehme, Gerry.
Title: John Lewis and desegregation / Gerry Boehme.
Description: New York : Cavendish Square Publishing, 2017. | Series: Primary sources of the civil rights movement | Includes bibliographical references and index.
Identifiers: LCCN 2016003672 (print) | LCCN 2016006765 (ebook) | ISBN 9781502618689 (library bound) | ISBN 9781502618696 (ebook)
Subjects: LCSH: Lewis, John, 1940 February 21---Juvenile literature. | African American civil rights workers--Biography--Juvenile literature. | Civil rights workers--United States--Biography--Juvenile literature. | African American legislators--Biography--Juvenile literature. | Legislators--United States--Biography--Juvenile literature. | African Americans--Civil rights--History--20th century--Juvenile literature. | Civil rights movements--Southern States--History--20th century--Juvenile literature.
Classification: LCC E840.8.L43 B64 2017 (print) | LCC E840.8.L43 (ebook) | DDC 328.73/092--dc23
LC record available at http://lccn.loc.gov/2016003672

Editorial Director: David McNamara
Editor: Fletcher Doyle
Copy Editor: Nathan Heidelberger
Art Director: Jeffrey Talbot
Designer: Amy Greenan
Production Assistant: Karol Szymczuk
Photo Research: J8 Media

Printed in the United States of America

CONTENTS

Equality and the Right to Vote

T he United States was founded upon the promise of freedom and equal rights for all. One of those rights was the ability to choose leaders who would serve all citizens.

When the American colonies claimed their independence from Great Britain in 1776, the second paragraph of their Declaration of Independence declared that:

> ... all men are created equal, that they are endowed by their Creator with certain unalienable Rights, that among these are Life, Liberty and the pursuit of Happiness.—That to secure these rights, Governments are instituted among Men, deriving their just powers from the consent of the governed.—That whenever any Form of Government becomes destructive of these ends, it is the Right of the People to alter or to abolish it, and to institute new Government.

American civil rights leader Martin Luther King Jr. walks with his wife, Coretta, while leading a march for equal voting rights in Alabama in March 1965.

At the time, the message seemed clear. Men are equal. Their rights, granted by a higher power, include freedom and the pursuit of a good life. A government draws its power from the citizens it is meant to serve. And, if the government fails in its mission, the people have a right to change it.

Unfortunately, right after the Declaration of Independence was signed, the debate began. Did *all men* include all *people*, or just men but not women? Did *all* really mean *all*, or just whites, to the exclusion of blacks, Native Americans, and other people of color?

Like many other countries at that time, the American colonies practiced slavery. Some of the men who signed the declaration believed that allowing slavery directly contradicted the idea of liberty. Others disagreed, especially those from the Southern colonies. Some owned slaves themselves and depended on the free labor that slaves provided. Some also felt deep racial **prejudice** and considered slaves to be "property," not human beings.

Just eleven years later, the United States Constitution guaranteed citizens the right to vote, but each state was

Congressman John Lewis stands on the Edmund Pettus Bridge in Selma, Alabama, fifty years after he and other civil rights marchers were viciously beaten by state troopers.

allowed to decide who could actually cast a ballot. While the requirements varied from one state to the next, all states allowed only white adult males to vote. African-American men—and all women—were excluded.

When the Civil War ended and slavery was abolished in 1865, the US Congress passed three constitutional amendments that guaranteed blacks freedom, citizenship, and the right to vote. In addition, two new acts (passed in 1866 and 1875) gave blacks more legal rights and outlawed discrimination based on a person's color in public transportation, facilities, and restaurants.

Southern states were still determined to limit the rights of black Americans, however. White Southerners passed laws that separated whites from blacks and made it difficult for African Americans to vote. For the next hundred years, the people of the **civil rights** movement fought in a life-or-death struggle against those opposed to equal rights for African-American citizens. The battle was filled with stories of bravery and dedication, suffering and sadness, faith, hope, and victory.

John Lewis joined that struggle as a young man in the early 1960s. He quickly became one of the most important leaders of his generation.

An Activist in the Making

Famous civil rights leader and congressman John Lewis was born on February 21, 1940, outside of Troy, Alabama. Troy was a small city in Pike County, an area known for its rich farmland. Pike County's population was only about thirty-two thousand when Lewis was born, and about half the people living there were African American. Typical for that time, most white people lived in or near the town, while most African Americans lived in the rural areas outside of town.

Happy but Poor

Lewis's parents were **sharecroppers**. John was the third of ten children. He grew up on his family's farm, working in the fields with his parents, three sisters, and six brothers. The family lived in a small, three-room house that had no running water and no electricity, and John shared a bed with two or

John Lewis grew up poor, living on a farm like this one in Alabama. As a child, he split his time between working with his family in the fields and attending school.

three of his brothers. Early in his life, the only book in his home was the Bible.

Recalling the days of his early childhood, Lewis said, "The world I knew as a little boy was a rich, happy one … We were poor—dirt poor—but I didn't realize it. It was a small world, a safe world, filled with family and friends."

Lewis's first school also lacked most modern conveniences. It had no playground, no furnace, no running water, and no bathrooms. The building had only two teachers and two rooms, with three grades sitting in each. All the students were black.

John's parents raised their children to respect all people and religions. They believed in the importance of education, but they also stressed the need for their children to work hard on the farm. Sometimes his parents got upset when Lewis wanted to go to school instead of working in the fields.

Lewis respected his parents, and he knew that the family needed his help on the farm, but he was also convinced that education would help him improve his life. In his book, *Walking with the Wind: A Memoir of the Movement*, Lewis spoke powerfully about how difficult it was to choose between school and working with his family:

> I was absolutely committed to giving everything I had to bettering myself in the classroom. I had no doubt that there was a way out of the world I saw around me and that this was the way. My parents, like most poor black parents of that time, agreed. To them as well, education represented an almost **mythical** key to the kingdom of America's riches, the kingdom so long denied to our race … [But] my parents needed my hands and my muscles, and as much as it hurt them, knowing how I adored school, they insisted I had to stay home … to help with the crops.

John Lewis attended schools for blacks only, such as this one. White schools usually had better teachers and facilities than those for blacks.

Some mornings, Lewis would hide from his parents until the school bus came, then sneak aboard so he could go to class. His father would scold him when he returned, but Lewis said that "Deep inside I think he knew there was no stopping me, that this was a decision I made about my life and that once I made a decision, it was just about impossible to turn me away from it. That's something that would remain true about me my entire life."

Before the 1960s, many businesses in the South had separate entrances and seating areas for white and African American customers.

Separate but Not Equal

Lewis's determination to improve his life grew stronger as he experienced life in the South as an African American. John Lewis grew up in a world where blacks and whites were kept separate. He traveled more than 20 miles (32 kilometers) by bus to attend his next public school, which also had only black students. While riding the bus each day, he passed by another school, located much closer to his house, which was reserved for white students only. He could see that it had better facilities, but he was not allowed to attend it because of his race.

Everywhere he went, Lewis was reminded that blacks were treated differently than whites. When he used public facilities like bathrooms, buses, and even water fountains, he saw signs that reserved some locations and seats for whites only, while other areas were designated for the use of blacks only.

Lewis was even denied a library card since African Americans were forbidden from borrowing books. Showing the determination that would later become his trademark, Lewis organized a **petition** to allow African Americans to take out books from the library, but the library ignored his request.

What John Lewis and other African Americans experienced was something called segregation, the separation of racial groups. Even though black and white citizens were supposed to be treated equally under the US Constitution, Southern states had passed laws that prevented African Americans from using the same resources as whites. In those days, the policies and laws that separated blacks from whites were referred to as "Jim Crow."

Belief in Change

As a young boy, Lewis was inspired by several experiences that made him think he could work to change life for African Americans. When he was eleven, he took a trip to Buffalo, New York, to visit some relatives. In his book *Finding Your Roots*, author Henry Louis Gates Jr. quotes Lewis describing how visiting Buffalo affected him:

> I saw another world, a different world. I saw black and white people living together, eating together in restaurants, at lunch counters. I rode an elevator for the first time, went in a very large department store for the first time. And I knew that it was different. It's better.

At school, he read books about famous black Americans like educator Booker T. Washington and champion boxer

Joe Louis. He read about Harriet Tubman and how she helped Southern slaves escape from their owners and get their freedom before and during the Civil War. He also learned about new laws that promised to give black Americans equal treatment to whites.

In 1954, a case called *Brown v. Board of Education of Topeka* reached the US **Supreme Court.** A young African-American girl named Linda Brown had been told she could not attend her local elementary school in Topeka, Kansas, because of the color of her skin. She was sent instead to a "separate but equal" school for black children. Lewis remembered feeling the same way when he was forced to take a long bus ride past a better school that was reserved for white students only.

White high school students gather around a radio in Georgia on May 17, 1954, to hear that the US Supreme Court ended segregation in public schools.

Brown's parents felt that she should be able to attend her local school and **sued** the school district. The National Association for the Advancement of Colored People (**NAACP**)

Jim Crow and Segregation

Although slavery ended in the United States in 1865, some people continued to believe that African Americans should not have equal rights. This feeling was especially strong in Southern states that supported slavery before the Civil War.

Civil rights protesters picketed businesses that practiced Jim Crow policies.

Beginning in the late 1870s, Southern states passed laws requiring whites to be separated from "persons of color" in public facilities including buses, trains, schools, parks, theaters, and restaurants to prevent contact between blacks and whites. In 1896, a US Supreme Court case known as *Plessy v. Ferguson* allowed segregation if the facilities were "separate but equal."

People used the **derogatory** term "Jim Crow" to refer in a negative way to black Americans, the policy of racial segregation in the South, and the laws that enforced it. Jim Crow was a character in an 1800s **minstrel show**. In such performances, the actors were white, but they blackened their faces and made fun of African Americans.

The Supreme Court later overturned *Plessy v. Ferguson* in 1954, paving the way for the civil rights movement to begin in earnest.

Many Southern whites resisted efforts to allow African Americans to attend schools that had previously been white-only.

supported Linda's case, and four similar cases, arguing that the black school was not "equal" to the white school because the white school had better facilities and was miles closer to her home. On May 17, the Supreme Court decided that racial segregation in public schools was "inherently unequal" and therefore always unconstitutional. This was a major victory for civil rights against Jim Crow laws.

Brown v. Board of Education helped to spark the civil rights movement of the 1950s and 1960s. While the case itself dealt only with public schools, people working for equal rights began to apply the idea that racial segregation was "inherently unequal and unconstitutional" to other public facilities as well.

The *Brown* case motivated Lewis to look for news about other situations involving equal rights for African Americans. In December 1955, when Lewis was fifteen years old, he heard about a woman named Rosa Parks, who refused to give up her seat on a bus in Montgomery, Alabama, to a white passenger. When she was arrested, African-American bus riders organized a **boycott** and refused to ride Montgomery buses. The bus boycott lasted for 381 days until the protesters finally won the right to be treated equally on the bus.

Inspired by Others

Lewis was also inspired by the words of Martin Luther King Jr., one of the leaders of the Montgomery bus boycott. Lewis first heard King's speeches on the radio. King preached the value of nonviolent protest, where people would refuse to obey laws that they felt were unjust but they would do so without violence. That included not fighting back when they were threatened, attacked, or arrested.

Lewis also saw that black leaders like King were inspired by their religion to devote their lives to pursuing social justice. Lewis also felt very strongly about how religion could be used to obtain equal rights for African Americans. He decided to become a minister and use religion as a powerful tool for change.

According to author Fred Powledge, Lewis later explained:

> I had come to resent segregation and discrimination at an early age. We had the poor schools, the run-down school buses, the unpaved roads; and I saw that those were penalties imposed on us because of race. So race was closely tied to my decision to be a minister … I wanted to use the emotional energy of the black church to end segregation and gain freedom for black people.

Even though he was naturally shy and spoke with a slight stammer, John Lewis began to preach in Baptist churches in the area. After becoming the first person in his family to graduate from high school, he moved to Nashville, Tennessee, to study at the American Baptist Theological Seminary.

Lewis then tried to enter an all-white college, Troy State College in Alabama, but was rejected due to his race. That made him even more determined to get involved in the cause of civil rights.

The Power of Nonviolence

Lewis enrolled at Fisk University in Nashville. While there, he began to follow the methods of James Lawson, a Methodist clergyman and activist who firmly believed in using the power of nonviolent protests to accomplish goals. Lawson had once traveled to India to study how the great Indian leader **Mohandas Gandhi** used nonviolent protests to achieve his country's independence from Great Britain.

Deeply religious, Lawson once described his belief in nonviolent protest in this way:

> When you are a child of God … you try to imitate Jesus, in the midst of evil. Which means, if someone slaps you on the one cheek, you turn the other cheek, which is an act of resistance. It means that you do not only love your neighbor, but you recognize that even the enemy has a spark of God in them, has been made in the image of God and therefore needs to be treated as you, yourself, want to be treated.

John Lewis was strongly affected by Lawson and his belief in the principle of nonviolence. These were, Lewis said, "incredibly powerful ideas … We were being trained for a war unlike any this nation had seen up to that time, a nonviolent struggle that would force this country to face its conscience."

John Lewis would soon combine his determination and strong religious values with the principles of nonviolence to become one of the most important leaders of the civil rights movement.

CHAPTER TWO

The Fight for Rights

During his first year at American Baptist Theological Seminary (now called American Baptist College) in Nashville, Tennessee, John Lewis concentrated on his studies and on becoming a minister. As he listened to the words of people like Martin Luther King, however, Lewis began to feel more strongly that Christians should live their faith by taking action against the pain and suffering that people experienced in real life. "It was that sense of mission, of involvement, of awareness that others were putting themselves on the line for the cause," Lewis said, that motivated him to get directly involved in civil rights causes.

Lewis began to attend workshops with other young activists. Guided by people like Jim Lawson, the group discussed ways that they could create something called the "beloved community," a place where people of different backgrounds accept that everyone is interconnected and that any person's well-being is linked to the well-being of others. They decided to take action to protest unequal treatment in their own city.

While Nashville was less segregated than other Southern cities at that time, African Americans were still separated from whites in many public places. When Lewis and his group asked Nashville blacks what form of segregation bothered them the most, their overwhelming response was segregated lunch counters in downtown stores. They could shop alongside whites, they said, but they could not sit in the same seats to eat. They felt that was humiliating and insulting.

In 1960, Lewis organized sit-in demonstrations at segregated lunch counters in Nashville. Black students would take seats in the "white only" sections and refuse to move. According to news reporter and writer David Halberstam, when some of his fellow activists told Lewis that they were afraid to join the protest, he answered them by saying:

> If not us, then who? Will there be a better day
> for it tomorrow, or next year? Will it be less
> dangerous then? Will someone else's children
> have to risk their lives instead of us risking ours?

To ensure that the sit-ins would go according to plan, Lewis and Bernard LaFayette printed leaflets in 1960 with the rules of nonviolent protest. The leaflets carried the following instructions:

```
RULES OF NONVIOLENT PROTEST

DO NOT:

1. Strike back nor curse if abused.
2. Laugh out.
3. Hold conversations with floor walker.
```

4. Leave your seat until your leader has given you permission to do so.
5. Block entrances to stores outside nor the aisles inside.

DO:

1. Show yourself courteous and friendly at all times.
2. Sit straight; always face the counter.
3. Report all serious incidents to your leader.
4. Refer information seekers to your leader in a polite manner.
5. Remember the teachings of Jesus Christ, Mahatma Gandhi, and Martin Luther King. Love and nonviolence is the way.

When the sit-ins began, some white Nashville residents reacted harshly. Protesters were harassed, beaten, arrested, and even jailed. However, Lewis and others in his group continued their nonviolent demonstrations. In *Walking with the Wind: A Memoir of the Movement,* John Lewis himself described the scene when some of the protesters were attacked as a television crew filmed it all:

> Yellow mustard was squeezed onto the head of one black male student … while the crowd hooted and laughed. Ketchup was poured down the shirt of another … [Another] was pulled off of his stool, beaten, and kicked by a group of young whites … A television camera crew was [there], recording the scene as [the] attackers spent themselves. It filmed [him]—bloody

and bruised and silent—pulling himself back on to his chair. When the footage aired that night on national television, it marked one of the earliest instances where Americans were shown firsthand the kind of anger and ugliness that the peaceful movement for civil rights was prompting in the South. Many viewers were sickened by what they saw. They would see more in the years to come.

Famous television newsperson Chet Huntley reported on the protests during an hour-long documentary for NBC News. Huntley said, "What we are witnessing today is a new kind of militancy and with it a new kind of soldier."

Eventually, Lewis joined with similar student groups across the South to form what became known as the Student

Former baseball star Jackie Robinson (*center*) joined a picket line in 1960 to protest discrimination against African Americans at Southern lunch counters.

John Lewis and Desegregation

Nonviolent Coordinating Committee (SNCC). The sit-ins continued for months and, over time, spread to more than one hundred cities across the South. It was during these sit-ins that John Lewis witnessed the true effectiveness and power of nonviolent protest. "Violence does beget violence," he said, "but the opposite is just as true. Hitting someone who does not hit back can last only so long. Fury spends itself pretty quickly when there's no fury facing it."

In April 1960, Lewis and his allies finally won the support of Nashville's white mayor, and some stores began to open their lunch counters to diners of all races soon afterwards. The students then targeted their nonviolent protests against other segregated areas in the city, including stores and movie theaters.

Freedom Rides

Lewis and others next turned their attention to segregated seating on buses and trains. In 1961, the Congress of Racial Equality (CORE) organized a series of Freedom Rides. Their goal was to ride buses through the South, using whites-only waiting rooms and restrooms, to protest segregation. John Lewis was one of the volunteers on the first ride.

In Rock Hill, South Carolina, Lewis was viciously attacked by white men when he entered the whites-only waiting room. At a bus station in Montgomery, Alabama, Lewis was knocked to the ground unconscious when a white mob attacked the Freedom Riders. He suffered a gash on the back of his head.

The violence that the Freedom Riders experienced drew attention from around the country and the world. Howard K. Smith, a reporter for CBS News, described an assault on one of the riders by saying that a white mob "beat him and kicked him until his face was a bloody, red pulp." Many people viewed the attacks as an outrage against people who were only trying to follow the law.

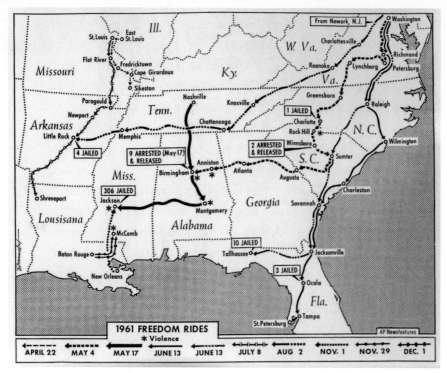

This map traces the routes of the Freedom Rides, which took place across the South from April through December 1961.

Others, however, had a different point of view. After the Montgomery police failed to protect the Freedom Riders from an angry mob, Police Commissioner L. B. Sullivan said, "We have no intention of standing guard for a bunch of troublemakers coming into our city making trouble." Alabama's governor at the time, John Patterson, declared that "We can't act as nursemaids to agitators. The state of Alabama can't guarantee the safety of fools." Alabama congressman George Huddleston Jr. said, "Every decent Southerner deplores violence. But these trespassers—these self-appointed merchants of racial hatred—got just what they deserved."

Even as Lewis and his followers were beaten, arrested and jailed, new Freedom Riders were driven to join the cause by what they had seen and heard. More than one thousand

Songs of Protest

During the early days of the civil rights movement, music served as a powerful unifying force. Protesters sang many songs that expressed their desire for freedom and better relations between the races. Perhaps the most famous was "We Shall Overcome."

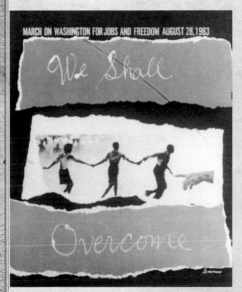

"We Shall Overcome" was used as a call to action for the March on Washington in 1963.

No one knows the true origin of "We Shall Overcome," but according to an article in the *Los Angeles Times*, a version written by folk singer and civil rights activist Guy Carawan soon became a rallying cry for activists across the country.

The first verse and chorus of "We Shall Overcome" express the resolve and the hope that civil rights workers felt about their cause and their eventual success:

We shall overcome
We shall overcome
We shall overcome some day
Oh, deep in my heart
I do believe
We shall overcome some day.

Later verses include the lyrics "We'll walk hand in hand," "We shall all be free," "We are not afraid," and "We are not alone." The Library of Congress called "We Shall Overcome" "the most powerful song of the 20th century."

Freedom Rider James Peck is attacked and beaten by a white mob at a bus station in Birmingham, Alabama, on May 14, 1961.

people made Freedom Rides during the summer of 1961. On September 22, 1961, the Interstate Commerce Commission (ICC) issued regulations that required depots to post notices that seating "is without regard to race, color, creed or national origin" and stated that bus companies would break the law if they sent buses to segregated stations. By the end of 1962, CORE declared that the battle against segregated travel had been won.

John Lewis said that the Freedom Rides were "more than just a ride for freedom. It was a ride meant to awaken the heart of America to the injustice of its own laws and traditions."

March on Washington

On August 28, 1963, Lewis delivered a powerful speech in front of more than one quarter of a million people gathered in Washington, DC. The rally was called the March on Washington for Jobs and Freedom. Organized by a number of civil rights and religious groups, the marchers pushed for passage of the Civil Rights Act, which was then stalled in

Congress. The march reached a climax with Martin Luther King Jr.'s "I Have a Dream" speech, which was a call for racial justice and equality.

Martin Luther King Jr. delivers his "I Have a Dream" speech on the National Mall during the March on Washington. John Lewis spoke shortly before King.

Voter Registration

The success of the Freedom Rides inspired people of all ages and races to work harder for civil rights. In addition to fighting segregation, civil rights leaders decided to focus on registering more African Americans to vote. That would help black citizens to claim a greater voice in choosing their leaders and changing laws that held them back.

Martin Luther King Jr. had said that "the central front is that of **suffrage**. If we in the South can win the right to vote, it will place in our hands ... the concrete tool with which we ourselves can correct injustice."

Southern states had passed laws that made it more difficult or even impossible for blacks to vote. They included poll taxes, difficult tests for reading and writing, and limiting the times when people could register. Even worse, registration officials could decide who passed and who failed the tests based on their own opinion. These conditions were applied to black voters but rarely to whites, in the hope that fewer blacks would actually be able to vote. Sometimes the names of African Americans who attempted to register were passed to violent whites, who would later find them and threaten them and their families.

In his memoir, Lewis said that:

> As we would soon learn, there was no separation between action and voter registration … Voter registration was as threatening to the entrenched white establishment in the South as sit-ins or Freedom Rides, and … it would prompt the same violent response.

Leaders in the US government, including President John F. Kennedy and his brother, Attorney General Robert (Bobby) Kennedy, also strongly suggested that the civil rights movement would be more effective for the long term if it focused on registering black voters rather than on demonstrations that could turn violent. President Kennedy had been elected with the help of African Americans who were able to vote in the 1960 election, and his administration pledged to provide financial support to voter education projects in the South.

In 1962, the SNCC began a program to register black voters in Mississippi. Registration increased over the next two years, but slowly. Out of five million blacks who were eligible to vote in the South in 1964, only two million (40 percent) had actually registered, and states like Alabama (less than 23 percent) had much lower participation.

In 1964, John Lewis coordinated SNCC efforts to organize voter registration drives and community action programs during the Mississippi Freedom Summer. The SNCC decided to use the same strategy that had worked so well in the past—organize peaceful civil rights protests, use any violence against the volunteers to attract the attention of the rest of the country, and force the US government to act.

Bloody Sunday

The following year, John Lewis was among the leaders of a march that became one of the most important moments of the civil rights movement. On March 7, 1965, Lewis and Hosea Williams, another dynamic civil rights leader, led more than six hundred protesters as they prepared to walk across the Edmund Pettus Bridge in Selma, Alabama. Their goal was to march from Selma to Montgomery to demand equal voting rights in the state.

Alabama governor George Wallace issued an order to prohibit the march, saying it "cannot and will not be tolerated." Despite the order, the protesters gathered at the Brown Chapel African Methodist Church and left to begin their march to Montgomery. As they approached the Edmund Pettus Bridge, their path was blocked by about one hundred state troopers, as well as another group of local lawmen, some of them on horseback. Within minutes, the troopers and local lawmen violently attacked the marchers with clubs, tear gas, metal chains, and electric cattle prods.

Witness and journalist Roy Reed described the attack in a March 8, 1965, article in the *New York Times*:

> The troopers stood shoulder to shoulder in a line across both sides of the divided four-lane highway. They put on gas masks and held their nightsticks ready as the **Negroes** approached, marching two abreast, slowly and silently ... The troopers rushed forward, their blue uniforms and white helmets blurring into a flying wedge

as they moved … The first 10 or 20 Negroes were swept to the ground screaming, arms and legs flying … The mounted [lawmen] spurred their horses and rode at a run into the retreating mass. The Negroes cried out as they crowded together for protection and the whites on the sideline whooped and cheered … Suddenly there was a report, like a gunshot, and a gray cloud spewed over the troopers and the Negroes. "Tear gas!" someone yelled. Two other witnesses said they saw [lawmen] using whips on the fleeing Negroes as they recrossed the bridge … From the hospital came a report that the victims had suffered fractures of ribs, heads, arms and legs, in addition to cuts and bruises.

John Lewis suffered a fractured skull, and more than fifty other marchers required emergency treatment and even hospitalization. According to Reed, Hosea Williams said, "I fought in World War II, and I once was captured by the German army, and I want to tell you that the Germans never were as inhuman as the state troopers of Alabama."

News cameras captured the brutality and violence of what became known as "Bloody Sunday" and quickly spread the news around the world. Leaders in Congress reacted angrily, with New York Senator Jacob Javits referring to the troopers' actions in Selma as an "exercise in terror." Days later, US president Lyndon Johnson said at a news conference:

What happened in Selma was an American tragedy. The blows that were received, the blood that was shed … must strengthen the determination of each of us to bring full equality and equal justice to all of our people. This is not just the policy of your government or your

State troopers attack John Lewis (*on his knees in the foreground*) and other voting rights marchers in Selma, Alabama, on March 7, 1965.

president. It is the heart and the purpose and the meaning of America itself.

The violence of Bloody Sunday forced the US government to act. One week later, when Martin Luther King Jr. led 3,000 protestors on a five-day march to Montgomery, they were protected by 1,800 armed Alabama National Guardsmen, 2,000 US Army troops, 100 FBI agents, and 100 US marshals.

On Monday, March 15, just eight days after Bloody Sunday, President Johnson spoke in front of a joint session of Congress to request the passage of a new voting rights bill. Johnson compared Selma to other important dates in US history, such as the first shots fired at Lexington and Concord that began the American Revolution and the surrender of the Confederates that ended the Civil War. Johnson ended his speech by quoting the title and first line from the famous protest song used by the civil rights demonstrators for inspiration: "We Shall Overcome!"

Johnson signed the Voting Rights Act into law on August 6, 1965, just five months after the tragic events of Bloody Sunday.

CHAPTER THREE

The Pinnacle of the Civil Rights Movement

When President Lyndon Baines Johnson signed the Voting Rights Act (VRA) on August 6, 1965, he spoke about the importance of the right to vote in his speech to Congress and others.

"The vote is the most powerful instrument ever devised by man for breaking down injustice and destroying the terrible walls which imprison men because they are different from other men," he said.

He also said, "Millions of Americans are denied the right to vote because of their color … This law covers many pages. But the heart of the act is plain. Wherever, by clear and objective standards, states and counties are using regulations, or laws, or tests to deny the right to vote, then they will be

President Lyndon Johnson signs the landmark 1965 Voting Rights Act. The act abolished methods that states had used to keep legal residents from voting, and it guaranteed the right to vote for all citizens.

struck down. If it is clear that State officials still intend to discriminate, then Federal examiners will be sent in to register all eligible voters."

Johnson also called on African-American leaders, who had already worked so hard and sacrificed so much, to continue their efforts to make sure that black Americans took advantage of this new opportunity. "This act is not only a victory for Negro leadership," Johnson said. "This act is a great challenge to that leadership. It is a challenge which cannot be met simply by protests and demonstrations. It means that dedicated leaders must work around the clock to teach people their rights and their responsibilities and to lead them to exercise those rights and to fulfill those responsibilities and those duties to their country."

Positive Effects

The Voting Rights Act of 1965 made immediate impact. It banned racial discrimination and secured equal voting rights for each citizen. It restored the right to vote guaranteed by the Fourteenth and Fifteenth Amendments to the Constitution, which say that no state shall abridge the privileges of US citizens and that no one can be denied the right to vote because of race. It also eliminated the use of unfair literacy tests, poll taxes, and other practices that stopped people from registering and voting. In his book *Give Us the Ballot: The Modern Struggle for Voting Rights in America*, author Ari Berman wrote that the act "quickly became known as the most important piece of civil rights legislation in the twentieth century and one of the most transformational laws ever passed by Congress."

African-American leaders took up President Johnson's challenge to get to work to implement black voter registration. In Mississippi, black registration went from less than 10 percent in 1964 to almost 60 percent in 1968. Alabama's percentages rose from 24 to 57 percent over the same four years. About one million black Southerners registered to vote within a few years after the VRA passed. Now able to go to the polls, large numbers of African Americans exercised their new right to vote and elected scores of local and state representatives.

The civil rights actions of the early 1960s also helped African Americans make great strides in other areas of American life. The sit-ins, demonstrations, and Freedom Rides changed how black Americans traveled, where they ate, and even where they lived. Some African Americans took advantage of greater integration in education and housing to attend better schools and move into nicer neighborhoods.

This cartoon was published two days after President Lyndon Johnson asked Congress for a Voting Rights Act in March 1965. It pokes fun at literacy tests that Southern states used to restrict voting rights for African Americans.

A substantial black middle class arose, in both the North and the South.

Whites Affected, Too

When the Civil Rights Act passed, life for whites in the South changed as well. In an article about how white southerners reacted to the age of civil rights, author Jason Sokol wrote:

Suddenly, whites had to serve blacks in their
stores and dine beside them at restaurants.
Such changes shattered the rhythm of white
southerners' daily lives. Many whites denounced
the "Civil Wrongs Bill," holding that such
federal laws imperiled their own rights. They
clung to the notion that rights were finite,
and that as blacks gained freedom, whites
must suffer a loss of their own liberties … The
Voting Rights Act granted African Americans a
stunning new power. In these citadels of the old
slave South, where whites were outnumbered by
a ratio of almost four-to-one, blacks voted some
of their own into political office.

Some whites reacted with violence, still participating
in secret hate groups like the Ku Klux Klan. Others felt a
sense of relief, finally freed from the guilt they felt over the
segregation and bad treatment they saw African Americans
endure every day. In the end, the civil rights movement
transformed the South and the nation.

Over the course of the struggle, the civil rights movement
itself had changed as well. The leadership had been tested and
strengthened through the demonstrations and the jail time
that followed. More young people were attracted to the cause,
and more whites and Southerners joined as well.

Jim Zwerg was a white twenty-one-year-old student from
Wisconsin who became a Freedom Rider and was savagely
beaten in Montgomery as a "race traitor." In his forward to
author Ann Bausum's book about the Freedom Riders, Zwerg
described why he joined the protest:

Why did I participate in the Freedom Rides?
The answer is simple. It was the right thing to
do. When I and other students in Nashville

learned about the attacks on the first Freedom Riders, we knew we could not permit violence to defeat social progress ... Was I scared? Yes. But there are some things worth putting your life on the line for. I knew our cause was right and just ... I was never so certain that I was living my faith as God intended ... We were part of a nationwide force for change, driven by the power of love, faith and destiny.

The end of legal segregation in the South had unexpected consequences as well, with some of them affecting African Americans in negative ways.

As blacks had more opportunities to attend better schools that were previously white-only, all-black schools lost some of their better students, especially traditionally all-black universities. Some black-owned businesses suffered as their African-American customers shopped in white-owned stores. More blacks got jobs in white companies, and some who were better off financially moved to nicer neighborhoods where they had previously been excluded. As a result, some black communities suffered and lost important role models and leaders.

The Movement Splits

The changing conditions also affected the civil rights movement. Some younger civil rights activists began to criticize established leaders like Martin Luther King Jr. and John Lewis for continuing to plan big demonstrations, marches, and speeches rather than focus on getting small things done on the local level. Different organizations and leaders began to compete for attention, volunteers, and funding. Author James Haskins wrote, "They began to work separately, pursuing different goals and jealously guarding their individual campaigns."

Segregation and the Vote

The struggle for civil rights and the vote pitted African Americans and their allies against Southern white segregationists. Both sides argued passionately for their cause.

Senator James Eastland from Mississippi was a staunch supporter of segregation.

United States Senator James Oliver Eastland, a Democrat from Mississippi, strongly opposed both the civil rights movement and the Voting Rights Act. Addressing the Senate in 1954, he said:

[The] southern institution of racial segregation or racial separation was the correct, self-evident truth which arose from the chaos and confusion of the **Reconstruction** period. Separation promotes racial harmony. It permits each race to follow its own pursuits, and its own civilization. Segregation is not discrimination … It is the law of nature, it is the law of God, that … free men have the right to associate exclusively with members of their own race, free from governmental interference, if they so desire.

Eastland denied that the South restricted black voting rights in an interview with television reporter Mike Wallace in 1957. "Well, I have enough knowledge of those allegations to know that there's nothing to them … Our qualifications that are written in the law apply to all races alike."

President Lyndon B. Johnson hands a pen to Martin Luther King Jr. during the signing of the Voting Rights Act.

On March 5, 1965, President Lyndon Johnson delivered a powerful speech where he skillfully linked the right to vote with the broader issue of equal rights for all:

> Our fathers believed that if this noble view of the rights of man was to flourish, it must be rooted in democracy. The most basic right of all was the right to choose your own leaders … Every American citizen must have an equal right to vote … Yet the harsh fact is that in many places in this country, men and women are kept from voting simply because they are Negroes. Every device of which human ingenuity is capable has been used to deny this right … Experience has clearly shown that the existing process of law cannot overcome systematic and ingenious discrimination … The Constitution says that no person shall be kept from voting because of his race or his color. We have all sworn an oath before God to support and to defend that Constitution. We must now act in obedience to that oath.

The Vietnam War also caused tension. There were civil rights activists who insisted that the war pulled resources away from the war on poverty and injustice at home. Other activists wanted to keep the issues of civil rights in the United States and foreign policy separate.

In an even more major shift, some civil rights activists began to question the effectiveness of nonviolence. Some wanted change to happen faster and were frustrated with the politics of the established leaders. Others objected that whites were playing too big of a role in the movement. They felt that blacks alone should determine their own destiny.

Black Power

In 1966, Stokely Carmichael became the chairman of the SNCC. Carmichael was born in Trinidad but came to the United States as a young child. He was inspired to join the civil rights movement when he saw news reports of lunch counter sit-ins on television.

Carmichael called for "Black Power" and urged African Americans to arm themselves for self-defense. By taking that position, Carmichael sent a clear signal that he wanted to break away from the nonviolent methods championed by civil rights leaders like John Lewis and Martin Luther King Jr.

In his book *Walking with the Wind*, John Lewis says that the term "Black Power" had been used by writers and politicians for years, and that he and other civil rights workers used the slogan "Black power for black people" during their campaigns in Alabama. However, Lewis says that an SNCC staffer named Willie Ricks shortened the phrase to "Black Power" in speeches that he gave in Mississippi in 1966.

Lewis described Ricks as "brash, aggressive," and angry that a close friend had been killed during an earlier demonstration. Ricks "knew how to stir up a crowd," Lewis wrote. "He termed himself a black **nationalist**, and he was not at all interested in the philosophy of nonviolence or the

African-American civil rights activist H. Rap Brown raises his fist in the "Black Power Salute" during a protest march in 1967.

concept of a biracial community." Lewis goes on to say that Stokely Carmichael adopted the phrase "Black Power" for himself when he saw how strongly crowds responded to Ricks and his speeches.

In his 1968 book, *Black Power: The Politics of Liberation*, Carmichael explained what he meant by Black Power: "It is a call for black people in this country to unite, to recognize their heritage, to build a sense of community. It is a call for black people to define their own goals, to lead their own organizations."

Black Power also represented Carmichael's move away from the goal of racial integration. Instead, he wanted to

Black Power advocate Stokely Carmichael was a powerful speaker. He succeeded John Lewis as leader of the SNCC.

John Lewis and Desegregation

pursue black separatism, the idea that black Americans should separate themselves from whites and form their own society. While he talked about African Americans gaining economic and political power, many people thought he was also supporting black violence. That made many white Americans afraid, even those who previously supported the civil rights movement.

The moves to exclude whites and move away from nonviolence led many moderate members to leave the SNCC, including Lewis.

"I still had faith in the principles we had applied to the formation of [the] SNCC," Lewis wrote, "but [the] SNCC itself had now abandoned them. The organization was riddled with bitterness and talk of retaliation and violence … I felt I owed an allegiance to a higher principle than [the] SNCC, and so it was time for me to leave."

CHAPTER FOUR

Pointing the Way to Freedom

T he success of the civil rights movement in the 1960s depended on many different factors, all of which came together during that remarkable era. Thousands of people, black and white, of all ages and backgrounds, joined with one another in a call to action, many for the first time in their lives. Young students and religious ministers in particular gave the movement a strong sense of passion and power.

All three branches of the US government—the president, Congress and the Supreme Court—took specific actions that helped end segregation policies and supported voting rights across the country, especially in the Southern states that had separated blacks and whites for nearly a century. Television networks, newspapers, and magazines circulated stories and pictures about the struggle and its violence throughout the country and the world, turning public opinion in favor of the protesters.

The six leaders of the nation's largest national black organizations (the "Big Six") included (*from left*) John Lewis, Whitney M. Young Jr., A. Philip Randolph, Martin Luther King Jr., James Farmer, and Roy Wilkins.

One of the "Big Six"

John Lewis was a leader in the Nashville sit-ins and in the Selma march, and he was the youngest speaker at the lectern with Martin Luther King Jr. that day in August during the March on Washington. Lewis soon became recognized as one of the most important young leaders of the civil rights movement.

Bernard LaFayette, another civil rights activist at the time, had been roommates and best friends with John Lewis in college. In his book *In Peace and Freedom: My Journey in Selma*, LaFayette praised Lewis and his importance to the civil rights cause:

> John had been arrested many times in his
> activist career and always led from the front of
> the line, fearless and determined … He was one
> of the leaders of the Nashville sit-in movement,
> one of the original thirteen Freedom Riders, and

a valued associate of Dr. King's for many years. John was considered to be the most unlikely to survive the movement because when there was a call for a protest, he was first on the line, his chin slightly elevated, ready to walk.

By 1963, Lewis was referred to as one of the "Big Six" leaders of the civil rights movement. The others were James Farmer of CORE, Martin Luther King Jr. of the **SCLC**, Roy Wilkins of the NAACP, Whitney M. Young Jr. of the National Urban League, and A. Philip Randolph, founder of the Brotherhood of Sleeping Car Porters. Lewis is the last living member, and he is one of the few remaining leaders of the 1960s civil rights movement who is still an active and vocal force today.

Despite suffering numerous physical attacks, many serious injuries and more than forty arrests, John Lewis remained committed to the philosophy of nonviolence. After leaving the SNCC in 1966, Lewis moved to Atlanta, Georgia, and stayed active in the civil rights movement. He spent the next few years working on several organizing projects, including serving as the director of the Voter Education Project (VEP). Under his leadership, the VEP helped to add nearly four million minorities to the voter rolls.

Time to Get Elected

In 1977, President Jimmy Carter appointed Lewis to direct ACTION, the federal volunteer agency that included the Peace Corps and Volunteers in Service to America (VISTA). It was during this time that Lewis became frustrated trying to work with government officials in Washington, DC, and decided to run for office himself:

> I was seeing too much **bureaucratic** and political infighting all around me …
> Washington, unfortunately, is a city filled with

ambition, with individuals ... who are unwilling to take a chance, to take a risk, to think of anyone or anything else besides themselves and their own careers. I was not naïve. I knew how Washington works ... I was convinced now more than ever that I had to find a way to get elected to a position where I would have more control over the things I thought ought to be done ... I wanted to be one of those people doing the listening and the deciding.

President Barack Obama presents John Lewis with the 2010 Medal of Freedom during a ceremony in the White House on February 15, 2011.

Lewis returned to Atlanta and ran for public office, winning an election for Atlanta city councilman in 1981. He then was elected to Congress in November 1986 and has served as US representative of Georgia's fifth congressional district ever since, reelected nine times, often without any opposition. He has served in leadership positions in Congress and has received many honors, including the Martin Luther King Jr. Nonviolent Peace Prize and the John F. Kennedy Profile in Courage Award. In 2011, he received the Presidential Medal of Freedom.

Today's Challenges

The civil rights movement did bring about changes in American life. The days of segregated bus seats, lunch counters, and hotels faded into memory. Slowly but surely, white supremacist hate groups lost much of their power.

However, the years following the passage of the Voting Rights Act also brought some difficult times for race relations in America. When Martin Luther King Jr. was **assassinated** by white racist James Earl Ray in 1968, riots erupted in more than one hundred US cities. Fires destroyed neighborhoods in Washington, DC. More recently, a disturbing number of young African-American men have been shot by white police officers in cities across the nation, leading many to question the relationship between law enforcement agencies and the minority communities they are sworn to serve and protect.

Black Americans still have far to go to reach equality. African Americans are still more likely than whites to die in infancy, live in poverty, and drop out of school. Blacks also make less money for the same work, and many still live in primarily black neighborhoods.

Through the years, African American leaders have urged their followers to register and vote in local and national elections, using their power at the ballot box to elect representatives who will be more responsive to their needs and issues. Unfortunately, the right to vote that John Lewis and others fought so hard to attain has also come under recent attack.

Voting Rights—New Questions

Selma and the signing of the Voting Rights Act in 1965 stand out as landmarks of the civil rights movement. Howevers, while the VRA has existed for more than fifty years, the fight over voting rights continues today.

The Voting Rights Act of 1965 was designed to be a temporary fix for what was considered to be an emergency situation. Some regulations were originally intended to remain for only five years. However, the Justice Department believed that racial barriers to voter registration continued to exist, so provisions in the act were renewed by Congress four times—

Voting Rights Still an Issue

In recent years, many states have passed laws that make it more difficult to vote. They include requiring proof of citizenship or a government ID such as a driver's license to register, shutting down voter registration drives, limiting early voting, purging voter rolls, and forbidding ex-felons from voting. Many activists believe that these kinds of regulations target certain groups—young people, African Americans, Hispanics, women, and the poor—that helped to elect President Barack Obama and who tend to vote against traditional conservatives.

When the Supreme Court struck down provisions of the Voting Rights Act in 2013, Eric Holder, the first African American to become US attorney general, said that the decision represented "a serious setback for voting rights and has the potential to negatively affect millions of Americans across the country." The president of the NAACP, Benjamin Jealous, called these efforts "the greatest attack on voting rights since segregation."

John Lewis, who considers the Voting Rights Act one of his movement's biggest achievements, said he was "shocked, dismayed, disappointed. I take it very personally."

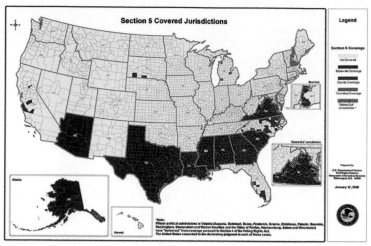

The above map shows the states (*in red*) and counties (*in blue*) that the US government marked for special treatment under the Voting Rights Act. These areas were determined to have policies that restricted voting rights.

in 1970, 1975, 1982, and in 2006—each time with updated regulations to address problems they found at that time.

In his book *Give Us the Ballot*, author Ari Berman writes that "the fight over the right to vote sharply intensified after Barack Obama's election" in 2008. Berman points out that Obama won three states from the former Confederacy, places where, as a black man, it would have been difficult, if not impossible, for him even to vote before 1965. Sadly, between 2010 and 2016, twenty-one states passed new laws that again made it more difficult for some people to vote.

Recently, the US Supreme Court made a decision that rolled back important parts of the Voting Rights Act. In June 2013, in the case *Shelby County v. Holder*, the court voted 5–4 to strike down key provisions of the VRA.

Sections 4 and 5 of the act had given the federal government the ability to reject new voting laws in certain states, mostly in the South, if it believed the laws discriminated against any group. In its 2013 decision, however, the Supreme Court decided that the VRA had worked so well that voting discrimination was no longer a serious problem

Supreme Court Justices John Roberts and Ruth Bader Ginsburg disagreed on *Shelby County v. Holder.*

in the South, and that it was unconstitutional to continue to interfere in state election laws.

Chief Justice John Roberts explained why he voted with the majority to strike down the key provisions:

In 1965, the states could be divided into two groups: those with a recent history of voting tests and low voter registration and turnout, and those without those characteristics.

Congress based its coverage formula on that distinction. Today the Nation is no longer divided along those lines, yet the Voting Rights Act continues to treat it as if it were.

Justice Ruth Bader Ginsburg, who voted against the decision, wrote a **dissenting** opinion, in which she said:

Congress approached the 2006 reauthorization of the VRA with great care and seriousness. The same cannot be said of the Court's opinion today. The Court makes no genuine attempt to engage with the massive legislative record that Congress assembled. Instead, it relies on increases in voter registration and turnout as if that were the whole story … The Court appears to believe that the VRA's success in eliminating the specific devices [in existence] in 1965 means that preclearance is no longer needed … With that belief, and the argument derived from it, history repeats itself.

New Efforts

In June 2015, on the second anniversary of the *Shelby County v. Holder* decision, congressional Democrats introduced new legislation to restore important provisions of the VRA. Then, in August, on the fiftieth anniversary of the Voting Rights Act, President Obama called on Congress to bring the law up to date and urged people to register to vote. "There are people of goodwill on both sides of the aisle who are willing to do it, but it keeps slipping as a priority," Obama said. "This has to be a priority."

In July 2015, Lewis wrote about this latest attack on the cause of voting rights that he holds so dear:

> Across the country, there is a deliberate, systematic attempt to make it harder and more difficult for the disabled, students, seniors, minorities, poor and rural voters to participate in the democratic process. We must not let that happen … The right to vote is the most powerful, nonviolent tool we have in a democratic society. My own mother, father, grandparents, and great-grandparents could not register to vote. My father died before he was ever able to cast a vote in this country. We must not slip back to that dark past.

The following September, Senator Lisa Murkowski of Alaska became the first Republican to cosponsor legislation by saying:

> The Voting Rights Act of 1965 brought an end to the ugly Jim Crow period in American history. It is fundamentally important in our

A man holds a protest sign at a 2015 rally in Winston-Salem, North Carolina, during a federal voting rights trial challenging a 2013 state law.

system of government that every American be given the opportunity to vote, regardless of who they are, where they live, and what their race or national origin may be.

When Barack Obama was inaugurated at the first African-American president of the United States, John Lewis said his election "is a sign. It is a symbol of progress we never even imagined was possible during the civil rights movement." But, he said, "We still have a distance to go before we join to create one nation, one people, one family—the American family. Until that day, the struggle continues."

John Lewis, an extraordinary man and leader, continues that struggle.

Chronology

Dates in green pertain to events discussed in this volume.

1863 The Emancipation Proclamation is issued by President Abraham Lincoln.

1865 The Thirteenth Amendment, abolishing slavery, is passed in the US House of Representatives. The amendment was passed by the Senate in 1864.

1868 The Fourteenth Amendment, guaranteeing equal rights under the law, is passed.

1870 The Fifteenth Amendment, prohibiting governments from denying male citizens the right to vote based on their race, is passed.

1883 The Supreme Court strikes down the Civil Rights Act of 1875, which guaranteed equal rights to all African Americans in transportation, restaurants or inns, theaters, and on juries.

1896 *Plessy v. Ferguson*, establishing the precedent of "separate but equal," is handed down by the Supreme Court of the United States.

1909 The National Association for the Advancement of Colored People (NAACP) is established.

1935 Thurgood Marshall and Charles Hamilton Houston successfully sue the University of Maryland, arguing for Donald Murray's admission to the institution's law school in *Murray v. Pearson*. The two argue that as the state does not provide a public law school for African Americans, it does not provide adequate "separate but equal" institutions.

1940 Civil rights leader and congressman John Lewis is born in Alabama.

1954 Thurgood Marshall and the NAACP win the case of *Brown v. Board of Education of Topeka*, which overturns *Plessy v. Ferguson* and the "separate but equal" doctrine of segregation in the United States.

1955 Rosa Parks refuses to give up her seat to a white person on a bus in Montgomery, Alabama. Her arrest sparks a bus boycott that leads to buses being desegregated in that city.

1957 Federal troops are called in to protect nine African-American students in Little Rock, Arkansas, who are trying to attend all-white Central High School.

1960–1961 John Lewis helps Nashville students organize sit-ins at lunch counters to protest segregation in restaurants; James Farmer leads CORE to organize the Freedom Rides to promote desegregation of buses and trains in the South. The riders suffer beatings from mobs.

1962 The Student Nonviolent Coordinating Committee (SNCC) begins to register black voters in Mississippi; US Supreme Court orders that African-American air force veteran James Meredith be allowed to enroll at the University of Mississippi.

1963 John Lewis is elected chairman of the SNCC and is named one of the Big Six leaders of the civil rights movement; Martin Luther King Jr. delivers his "I Have A Dream" speech to more than 250,000 people at the Lincoln Memorial in Washington, DC, during the March on Washington for Jobs and Freedom.

1964 President Lyndon B. Johnson signs the Civil Rights Act of 1964. John Lewis and the SNCC organize voter registration drives and community action programs during the "Mississippi Freedom Summer."

1965 John Lewis and others are attacked on a voting rights march by Alabama state troopers at the Edmund Pettus Bridge in Selma on Bloody Sunday; Martin Luther King Jr. leads march from Selma to Montgomery, Alabama; Voting Rights Act passes.

1966 John Lewis leaves the SNCC due to disagreements about moving away from the policy of nonviolence.

1967 Thurgood Marshall becomes the first African-American Supreme Court justice. The Supreme Court rules that laws prohibiting interracial marriage are unconstitutional.

1968 Martin Luther King Jr. is assassinated in Memphis, Tennessee. Shirley Chisholm becomes first African-American woman elected to Congress.

1977 President Jimmy Carter appoints John Lewis as an associate director of ACTION, a federal volunteer agency.

1981 John Lewis is elected to the Atlanta City Council.

2003 The Supreme Court upholds a policy at the University of Michigan Law School, ruling that race can be used as a consideration in admitting students.

2013 The Supreme Court overturns a component of the Voting Rights Act that states areas with a history of restricting voting rights must get pre-clearance before passing any voting laws that might affect minorities.

Glossary

assassinated Describing the murder of an important or famous person, usually in a surprise attack, for political or religious reasons.

boycott A refusal, usually by a large, organized group, to use the goods or services of a company, country, or public facility.

bureaucratic Describing a business or organization that makes decisions slowly, using too many rules and procedures instead of common sense.

civil rights The rights of people, especially African Americans, to receive equal treatment, to be free from discrimination, and to be protected under the law.

derogatory Insulting or disrespectful.

dissenting Disagreeing with an official decision.

minstrel show A stage show featuring songs, dances, and comic dialogue, usually performed by white actors in blackface, often making fun of African Americans.

Mohandas Gandhi Famous leader of the country of India who used nonviolent protest to win self-rule from Great Britain.

mythical From a fairy tale; magical or imaginary.

NAACP The oldest civil rights organization in the United States. Originally founded in 1909 as the National Association for the Advancement of Colored People, the full name is no longer used and the organization is referred to as the NAACP.

nationalist A person who wants political independence for a group or country. During the civil rights movement, some African Americans (black nationalists) wanted to create a separate country for blacks only.

Negroes A word that had been used to refer to a person of black ancestry or with dark skin. The term has been replaced by "black," "African American," or "person of color."

petition A written document that many people sign to show support for a person running for office or for a proposal.

prejudice An unfair feeling of dislike for a person or group based only on their race, sex, religion, or orientation.

Reconstruction The period (1865–1877) after the Civil War when the states that had seceded to form the Confederacy were controlled by the federal government before being allowed to rejoin the Union.

SCLC The Southern Christian Leadership Conference (SCLC) is an African-American civil rights organization. Its first president was Martin Luther King Jr.

sharecropper A farmer who works on land owned by someone else in return for a share of the crop's value after paying expenses.

sue Use a legal process to try to get a court of law to force a person, company, or organization that has treated you unfairly or hurt you in some way to give you something or to do something.

suffrage The right to vote in public elections.

Supreme Court The highest legal court in the United States.

Further Information

Books

Bausum, Ann. *Freedom Riders: John Lewis and Jim Zwerg on the Front Lines of the Civil Rights Movement*. Washington, DC: National Geographic Society, 2006.

Carrier, Jim. *A Traveler's Guide to the Civil Rights Movement*. Orlando, FL: Harcourt, Inc., 2004.

Feinstein, Stephen. *Inspiring African-American Civil Rights Leaders*. African-American Collective Biographies. Berkeley Heights, NJ: Enslow Publishers, Inc., 2013.

Lewis, John. *Walking with the Wind: A Memoir of the Movement*. Orlando, FL: Harcourt Brace & Company, 1998.

Orr, Tamra. *A History of Voting Rights*. Hockessin, DE: Mitchell Lane Publishers, 2013.

Websites

National Civil Rights Museum
civilrightsmuseum.org

The museum, located at the Lorraine Hotel, where Martin Luther King Jr. was assassinated, maintains a website with links to videos and articles that cover the gamut of the civil rights movement.

Website for Congressman John Lewis
johnlewis.house.gov/john-lewis
The official website of John Lewis, the only surviving member of the civil rights movement's Big Six, provides details on the political career of this courageous and decorated activist.

We Shall Overcome: Historic Places of the Civil Rights Movement
www.nps.gov/nr/travel/civilrights

The National Park Service provides stories about the civil rights movement, and maps and an itinerary for visiting historic sites where important events occurred.

Videos

Bloody Sunday 1965
www.history.com/topics/black-history/civil-rights-movement/videos/bloody-sunday-1965
The brutal attack on voting rights marchers in Selma, Alabama, is documented in this video from the History Channel.

John Lewis—Civil Rights Leader
www.history.com/topics/black-history/civil-rights-movement/videos/john-lewis--civil-rights-leader

The History Channel interviews historians and leaders of the civil rights movement about the impact of John Lewis.

Bibliography

Academy of Achievement. "John Lewis Biography." Last
modified March 17, 2015. Accessed December 19, 2015.
http://www.achievement.org/autodoc/page/lew0bio-1.

Benen, Steve. "Voting Rights Act Picks Up Unexpected GOP
Ally." MSNBC.com, September 11, 2015. http://www.
msnbc.com/rachel-maddow-show/voting-rights-act-picks-
unexpected-gop-ally.

Berman, Ari. *Give Us the Ballot: The Modern Struggle For
Voting Rights In America*. New York: Farrar, Straus and
Giroux, 2015.

Biography.com editors. "John Lewis—Civil Rights Activist,
US Congressman." Biography.com. Accessed December 21,
2015. http://www.biography.com/people/john-lewis-
21305903#civil-rights-struggle.

Biography.com editors. "Stokely Carmichael—Civil Rights
Activist." Biography.com. Accessed January 1, 2016.
http://www.biography.com/people/stokely-carmi-
chael-9238629#black-power.

Bullard, Sara. *Free At Last: A History of the Civil Rights
Movement and Those Who Died In the Struggle*. New York:
Oxford University Press, 1993.

Carpenter, Teresa. "John Lewis." In *Profiles in Courage for Our
Time*, edited by Caroline Kennedy. New York: Hyperion, 2002.

Colker, David. "Guy Carawan Dies at 87; Brought 'We
    Shall Overcome' to Civil Rights Movement." *Los Angeles
    Times*, May 7, 2015. Accessed December 30, 2015. http://
    www.latimes.com/local/obituaries/la-me-guy-carawan-
    20150507-story.html.

Ezra, Michael, ed. *Civil Rights Movement: People and
    Perspectives*. Santa Barbara, CA: ABC-CLIO, Inc., 2009

Gates, Henry Louis, Jr. *Finding Your Roots*. Chapel Hill, NC:
    The University of North Carolina Press, 2014.

Ginsberg, Ruth. "Ginsberg VRA Dissent." *Mother Jones*.
    Accessed January 2, 2016. http://www.motherjones.com/
    documents/717254-ginsberg-vra-dissent.

Harry Ransom Center. "Senator James Eastland: The Mike
    Wallace Interview." Harry Ransom Center: The University
    of Texas at Austin. Accessed January 5, 2016. http://www.
    hrc.utexas.edu/multimedia/video/2008/wallace/eastland_
    james_t.html.

Haskins, James. *Freedom Rides—Journey for Justice*. New York:
    Hyperion Books for Children, 1995.

History.com staff. "March On Washington." History.com.
    Accessed January 3, 2016. http://www.history.com/topics/
    black-history/march-on-washington.

"James Eastland." Project Gutenberg Self-Publishing Press. Accessed January 2, 2016. http://self.gutenberg.org/ articles/james_eastland#Views_on_civil_rights_and_race.

Keyssar, Alexander. *The Right To Vote: The Contested History of Democracy in the United States*. New York: Basic Books, 2000.

Korte, Gregory. "Obama Calls for Restoration of Voting Rights Act." *USA Today*, August 6, 2015. http://www. usatoday.com/story/news/politics/2015/08/06/obama-calls- restoration-voting-rights-act/31199889/.

LaFayette, Bernard, Jr. and Kathryn Lee Johnson. *In Peace and Freedom: My Journey in Selma*. Lexington, KY: The University Press of Kentucky, 2013.

Lewis, John. Forward to *A Traveler's Guide to the Civil Rights Movement*, by Jim Carrier, viii. Orlando, FL: Harcourt, Inc., 2004.

Meacham, Jon, ed. *Voices in Our Blood: America's Best on the Civil Rights Movement*. New York: Random House, Inc., 2001.

PBS. "Witness to Faith: John Lawson." This Far By Faith. PBS. Accessed January 2, 2016. http://www.pbs.org/this- farbyfaith/witnesses/james_lawson.html.

Reed, Roy. "Alabama Police Use Gas and Clubs to Rout Negroes." *New York Times*, May 18, 1965.

Roberts, John. "The Court Was Right to Strike Down Section 4 of the Voting Rights Act." In *Voting Rights*, edited by Noah Berlatsky. Opposing Viewpoints Series. Farmington Hills, MI: Greenhaven Press, 2015.

Sokol, Jason. "White Southerners' Reactions to the Civil Rights Movement." IIP Digital: US Department of State, December 29, 2008.http://iipdigital.usembassy.gov/st/english/publication/2009/01/20090106143801jmnamdeirf0.9369623.html#axzz3wLJx6fiE.

Wexler, Sanford. *The Civil Rights Movement: An Eyewitness History*. New York: Facts On File, Inc., 1993.

WGBH American Experience. "John Lewis: Freedom Rider." Freedom Riders, PBS. Accessed December 22, 2015. http://www.pbs.org/wgbh/americanexperience/freedomriders/people/john-lewis/.publication/2009/01/20090106143801jm-namdeirf0.9369623.html#axzz3wLJx6fiE.

Index

assassinated, 46

beloved community, 17–18
"Big Six," 43–44, **43**
Bloody Sunday, 27–29, **29**
boycott, 15
Brown, H. Rap, **39**
Brown v. Board of Education of Topeka, 12–14
bureaucratic, 44

Carmichael, Stokely, 38–39, **40**, 41
Civil Rights Act, 24–25, 33–34
CORE, 21, 24, 44

derogatory, 13
dissenting, 49

Eastland, James, 36, **36**
Edmund Pettus Bridge, **6**, 27–28

Fisk University, 16
Freedom Rides, 21–22, **22**, 24–26, **24**, 32, 34–35, 43

Gandhi, Mohandas, 16, 19

Jim Crow, 11, 13–14, **13**, 50
Johnson, Lyndon, 28–32, **31**, 37, **37**

Kennedy, John F., 26
King, Martin Luther, Jr., 5, 15, 17, 19, 25, 25, 29, 35, 37, 38, 43–44, **43**, 46
Ku Klux Klan, 34

LaFayette, Bernard, 18, 43–44
Lawson, James, 16–17
Lewis, John
  awards and honors, 45, **45**
  departure from SNCC, 35, 38–39, 41, 44
  early life, 7–12, **8**, **9**, 14–16
  Freedom Rides and, 21–22, 24
  legacy, 6, 43, 51
  March on Washington and, 24–25
  Nashville sit-ins and, 17–21
  political career, 44–45, 50–51
  religious beliefs, 15–17
  Selma march and, **6**, 27–28, **29**

voting rights and, 26–28,
44, 46–47, 50

March on Washington, **23**,
24–25, **25**, 43
minstrel show, 13
Montgomery bus boycott,
14–15
mythical, 9

NAACP, 12, 14, 44, 47
nationalist, 38
Negroes, 27–28, 31, 37
nonviolence, 15–16, 18–21,
27, 38, 41, 44–45, 50

Parks, Rosa, 14–15
petition, 11
Plessy v. Ferguson, 13
prejudice, 5

Reconstruction, 36
Ricks, Willie, 38–39
Robinson, Jackie, **20**

SCLC, 44
Selma march, 5, **6**, 27–29, **29**,
43, 46
sharecropper, 7
Shelby County v. Holder,
48–50, **49**
sit-ins, 18–21, 26, 32, 38, 43

slavery, 5–6, 12–13
SNCC, 21, 26–27, 38, **40**,
41, 44
sue, 12
suffrage, 25
Supreme Court, 12–14, 42,
47–50, **49**

Voter Education Project, 44
Voting Rights Act (VRA),
29–34, **31**, **33**, 36–37, **37**,
46–51, **48**

Washington, Booker T., 11
"We Shall Overcome," 23,
23, 29
Williams, Hosea, 27–28

About the Author

GERRY BOEHME is a published author, editor, speaker, and business consultant who was born in New York City. He loves to travel and to learn about new things and particularly enjoys talking with people who have different backgrounds and opinions.

Gerry has written several books for students dealing with various subjects, including dangerous drugs and famous people who have made a difference in other people's lives. He has also published many articles dealing with media, advertising, and new technology, and he has been featured as a speaker at business conferences across the United States as well as the United Kingdom, Australia, and the Republic of Korea.

Gerry graduated from the Newhouse School at Syracuse University and now lives on Long Island, New York, with his wife and two children.